The remarkable story of
Alfred Nobel and the

NOBEL PRIZE

Lars-Åke Skagegård

Translated by
George Varcoe

Konsultförlaget AB

Konsultförlaget AB
Box 867, S-751 08 UPPSALA
Sweden

Tel. + 46 18 15 50 80
Fax. + 46 18 15 50 85

Cover photo: William Sharpe, USA, receives his prize
from King Carl XVI Gustaf (1990)
Photo by Anders Holmström/Pressens Bild
Layout: Maria Johansson
Typesetting: Railey Publishing AB
Printed by Vällingby Reproduktion AB
Edition: 1:1
ISBN: 91-7005-049-X

Contents

Foreword

"In Sweden the Nobel Prize is big; in the rest of the world it's huge." That is how a visiting American described his and his countrymen's view of the Nobel Prize.

"It's the biggest and best export you have! But do you Swedes really understand that?"

Perhaps driven by the force of his question, I began to do some research into the subject.

Alfred Nobel was a shy man, misunderstood in love, with literary ambitions and an almost manic fear of death. Through his brilliant powers of invention and his good business sense he built the fortune which is the basis of today's prizes.

In his will, Alfred Nobel created a prize that is not only of considerable financial value, but also a sort of triumphal arch for all humanity. It rewards science, literature, and the quest for peace. It gives public recognition to the admirable results of individual endeavor.

The lives of the "laureates", or prizewinners, become somewhat of a modern fairy tale. They are thrust into the limelight out of relative anonymity. Many of them become prominent figures in the eternal struggle for a better and more humane world. With their contributions, people like Mother Teresa, Martin Luther King Jr., Alexander Fleming, Wilhelm Röntgen, etc. have demonstrated mankind's innate potential for creativity and divine good.

In an era of fast food and stock-market killings, the Nobel ceremonies let in a breath of fresh air. We need the calm and dignity they bring. We need the achievements and the awareness of the prizewinners and festival arrangers. We need that moment of encouragement.

I would like to thank those who have assisted in the production of this book, especially Lars Göran Andersson, general manager of the City Hall Restaurant for his valuable time and interest. Also to the Nobel Foundation, the Grand Hotel, Hässelby Flowers and the Swedish Post Office's Philatelic Section for their kind and knowledgeable help.

Uppsala, November 6, 1993

Lars-Åke Skagegård

Alfred Nobel

Alfred Nobel

Alfred Nobel died on December 10th 1896, leaving the major part of his fortune to a fund the annual income of which would be used to finance prizes of money to those who "shall have conferred the greatest benefit on mankind".

The Nobel Prizes were awarded for the first time in 1901. Since then, the prize has grown in prestige and respect. Who was Alfred Nobel — this man whose will has made his name immortal?

© The Nobel Foundation.

Alfred Nobel at the age of 50.

His parents were Immanuel and Andriette Nobel — a couple who were to experience both success and failure in life. Immanuel was a natural genius in mechanics, drawing and invention. He soon had a good reputation as an architect as well, but in 1833 the young family suffered a setback. As a result of a series of misfortunes, including a fire which razed their home, the family went bankrupt and was forced to move to a very spartan flat on the northern edge of Stockholm. The address was Norrlandsgatan 9.

1833 was also the year in which Alfred was born.

Bankruptcy was an extremely painful experience for the family. They still suffered from it many years later and it made a deep impression on the young Alfred. All his life he was to remember the insult and humiliation that his family suffered.

In 1937 Immanuel left the family to seek his fortune in the east. He traveled first to Turku, Finland, and then on to St. Petersburg to introduce his invention of explosive mines.

His wife Andriette remained in Sweden with the children, Robert, Ludwig and Alfred. The family had known the burden of poverty before, but now they were to experience an even harsher reality.

It was a difficult time for Andriette since she had to support her sons alone. But eventually good news came from Russia, to the effect that Immanuel had succeeded in convincing the Russians of the quality of his mines.

Now, in 1842, after five long years, the family could be reunited in St. Petersburg. Alfred was nine years old.

From having experienced deep poverty, Alfred was now a member of the upper class in a country where serfdom and mass poverty were part of everyday life. Immanuel was careful to ensure that his sons received a good education. At the age of 17 Alfred could already speak five languages fluently: Swedish, Russian, English, French and German.

Alfred soon showed great technical talent, but he also enjoyed reading books and, above all, writing.

When he began to write poems in earnest and expressed an ambition to become a writer, he met compact resistance from his father. Immanuel Nobel's plans for his son were not on the literary plane at all; he wanted Alfred to work on inventions and technology.

A planned study trip that would stretch over a long period and take in many countries was the weapon that his father used. If Alfred were to make the desired journey, he had to promise not to become a writer.

Alfred traveled to a number of European countries, but also to America where the 17-year old met, among others, Swedish inventor John Ericsson, builder of the ironclad warship Monitor. His father could not quench the fire in his son's heart, and Alfred continued to write poetry. But when he became a celebrity he dared not show his work in public, and later burned almost everything he had written. At the age of 63, however, Alfred Nobel published a play called "Nemesis". Perhaps he felt that his life was reaching an end, and he wanted, mainly for his own sake, to satisfy that writer's dream?

For Alfred's father Immanuel, business improved all the time and with it his finances. It was a time of war, and the Russian government needed large quantities of war materiel. They placed orders with Immanuel Nobel who thus made good profits and could pay all his debts in Sweden. For his contributions to Russian industry he was awarded the Imperial Gold Medal in 1853.

Immanuel experimented above all with various kinds of explosives, and Alfred followed in his footsteps.

During his long journey through Europe, Alfred had met an Italian in Paris, Ascanio Sobrero, who was experimenting with a material that had enormous explosive properties. Alfred realized at once the possibilities of nitroglycerine and he continued to develop the substance.

Alfred Nobel himself has described 1860 as the time when he "made nitroglycerine explode with success".

The rapid upheavals in the life of the Nobel family were far from over. Immanuel faced yet another bankruptcy. When the war was over, and thus the profitable munitions industry, he suffered large financial losses.

Once again the family was split, with Andriette Nobel and her youngest son Emil returning to Stockholm. A few years later Alfred also moved back to Sweden and, together with his father, continued his attempts to tame the new explosive.

In 1864 a disastrous accident occurred at the Nobel family estate, Heleneborg. In a shed in which the experiments were taking place, 140 kg of nitroglycerine exploded and five people were killed, among them Alfred's youngest brother Emil.

There were a number of accidents over the next few years. Many people tried to stop the dangerous experiments, but at the same time more and more were becoming aware of what enormous benefit the new explosive could bring. Alfred's main problem was to understand why nitroglycerine exploded so easily. He had to make it safe, so that lives were not put at risk every time it was used.

Finally he found the answer. By mixing nitroglycerine with a rare earth called kieselguhr, he could obtain an explosive force just as strong as before but much safer. He called the new discovery "dynamite".

Alfred obtained the sole right to manufacture dynamite in one country after another. In only a few years Alfred Nobel and his explosive had conquered the world.

In 1871 Alfred settled in Paris, where he bought a magnificent villa on the Avenue Malakoff. The house is still standing. Once there, he continued to experiment and succeeded in producing an even more effective explosive which he called "blasting gelatin".

In 1889 a macabre incident caused Alfred Nobel to have second thoughts. A journalist confused Alfred with his recently deceased brother Ludwig and Alfred could read his own obituary in the newspaper. In it, he was called the "merchant of death" because of all the profit he had made in improving weapons and developing explosives.

This hit Alfred very hard, since he was seriously trying to

Alfred Nobel, posthumous painting by Emil Österman.

invent weapons so terrible that their inhumanity would deter people from anything that had to do with war. He also donated considerable sums of money to peace organizations, and today these interests are reflected in the Nobel Peace Prize.

In time, Alfred Nobel became extremely wealthy and famous. He received vast numbers of invitations to receptions, but he usually refused them. Not, however, the President of France. Alfred considered it his duty to come when the President called.

Honors and awards were also part of his life. But throughout his life, Alfred Nobel maintained a healthy distance to himself and his fame. In 1893 he was given an honorary doctorate by the University of Uppsala, and he valued that particular honor very much.

While in France, Alfred tested his invention of the "Nobel igniter" on the French government's firing ranges.

He offered France the chance to purchase the rights to his invention, but they declined. Instead, Italy showed an interest and wanted to obtain his "Nobel igniter". Because of this, Alfred Nobel was accused of treason against France, and he felt forced to leave the country. His final home was the Italian town of San Remo, where he died on December 10th 1896.

Alfred Nobel was in many ways a divided, original personality. He never married or had children, and solitude was his constant companion.

This plagued him often, as did the meaninglessness of things. When his anxiety became unbearable, he would lock himself in his laboratory for several days in a row. His physical and mental upset gradually ebbed away in the intensity of his work.

Ever since childhood Alfred Nobel had suffered from weak health, often in the form of constant headaches, breathing difficulties, and heart problems.

He had a few love affairs during his journey through life, but the great inventor was never to know an all-encompassing love. As a young man he fell in love with a Swedish girl who worked as a pharmacist's assistant in Paris. Shortly after, the girl developed tuberculosis and died.

At the age of 43, Alfred Nobel advertised for an intelligent and mature woman who could fill the double role of companion and private secretary with a skill in foreign languages. He received an answer from 33-year old Bertha Kinsky. She had everything that Alfred was looking for. He could discuss matters with her as with an equal. With her intelligence and urbanity, her interest in literature and her linguistic talents, she was exactly the woman Alfred had sought for so long.

Bertha Kinsky was in love with an Austrian, Baron von Suttner, and was temporarily escaping from her own romance problems — the baron's parents would not accept her. When Alfred asked her if her "heart was free" she told him the truth, but Alfred was already in love.

Shortly afterward, when Alfred was away on a month-long business trip, she left only a brief message to say she had returned to her baron. After that, Alfred no longer believed he could awaken tender feelings in a "lady of the world". Instead, he felt he had become ridiculous. He sought solace with a young 18-year old flower girl — which sounds like a real-life Pygmalion story.

But a fairy tale is a fairy tale. Alfred did try to educate the girl by recommending books, but they remained two separate individuals with completely different attitudes and views of the world. For Sofie Hess, friendship with the aging Alfred Nobel meant having a fine home and new clothes.

The only woman who showed love for Alfred throughout his life was his mother Andriette. He was very fond of her and she always received a share when his business dealings were successful.

Alfred Nobel was haunted by a fear of death. Partly, it was a fear of being really dead, and partly being declared dead and then, after being buried, waking up in his own coffin. For that reason Alfred insisted that the veins in his wrists be opened after his death. Living alone, he also worried greatly about what his moment of death would be like. He did not want to die sur-rounded only by paid staff. It was important to have his friends and relatives there.

Alfred was struck by a brain hemorrhage and everything took place very quickly. What he had feared for so long now happened: he died alone, without friends, surrounded only by those who were paid to be there. A great inventor was gone, a man whose name will never be forgotten. In December of every year the name of Nobel is spread around the world in a spirit of festivity and dignity. Thanks to a man whose own life was in many ways a tragedy...

The Nobel Prize

The Nobel Prize

Alfred Nobel's last will and testament was remarkable in many ways. Friends and relatives received a good share of his fortune, but the larger portion, about 30 million Swedish kronor, went to a fund that would finance prizes of money to "those who, during the preceding year, shall have conferred the greatest benefit on mankind".

The amount of money was enormous. In today's currency it would be worth about one billion kronor (roughly $150,000,000). It became clear at once that this huge donation would cause some problems. In the first place, there were legal and formal complications. Nobel's wealth was to be found in a number of different countries, all of which had different laws. Moreover his relatives did their utmost to prevent the will from being approved. In addition to that, the will was not thought to be sufficiently patriotic. King Oscar II himself did what he could to stop it.

In his will, Nobel had insisted that "no consideration whatever shall be given to the nationality of the candidates, but that the most worthy shall receive the prize, whether he be a Scandinavian or not".

It soon turned out that the institutions which were named in the will to select the prizewinners had not been informed in advance.

With all the protests, contradictions, and problems, it was five years after Alfred Nobel died before the first prizes could be awarded, on December 10th 1901.

"The whole of my remaining realizable estate shall be dealt with in the following way: the capital, invested in safe securities by my executors, shall constitute a fund, the interest on which shall be annually distributed in the form of prizes to those who, during the preceding year, shall have conferred the greatest benefit on

mankind. The said interest shall be divided into five equal parts, which shall be apportioned as follows: one part to the person who shall have made the most important discovery or invention within the field of physics; one part to the person who shall have made the most important chemical discovery or improvement; one part to the person who shall have made the most important discovery within the domain of physiology or medicine; one part to the person who shall have produced in the field of literature the most outstanding work of an idealistic tendency; and one part to the person who shall have done the most or the best work for fraternity between nations, for the abolition or reduction of standing armies and for the holding and promotion of peace congresses. The prizes for physics and chemistry shall be awarded by the Swedish Academy of Sciences; that for the physiological or medical works by the Karolinska Institute in Stockholm; that for literature by the Academy in Stockholm, and that for champions of peace by a committee of five persons to be elected by the Norwegian Storting. It is my express wish that in awarding the prizes no consideration whatever shall be given to the nationality of the candidates, but that the most worthy shall receive the prize, whether he be a Scandinavian or not".

Excerpt from Alfred Nobel's will dealing with the Nobel Prize.

The part of Nobel's will that dealt with the prizes and those who should award them was not entirely uncontroversial. The literature prize should be awarded by the "Academy in Stockholm", which was interpreted to mean the Swedish Academy. They had to struggle with the delicate formulation "the person who shall have produced in the field of literature the most outstanding work of an idealistic tendency".

The fifth prize, for the furtherance of peace, was to be awarded by the Norwegian Parliament. This was a sensation. Sweden and Norway formed a union at that time, but voices were increasingly being raised in Norway against the union and for a free Norway. To allow the Peace Prize to be awarded in Oslo in those times of unrest seemed risky.

However, it all turned out the way Alfred Nobel wanted.

The money

The prestige of the Nobel Prize is unique in the world. For the prizewinner it means change. After perhaps working in relative anonymity for years, the laureate is suddenly in the spotlight. The Nobel Prize is the most significant prize a scientist, writer, or promoter of peace can receive. The honor is invaluable, and the money is considerable too.

The actual sum has varied greatly. The first year it amounted to 150,000 kronor. But since the Nobel Foundation was tied to regulations limiting the placing of capital, the amount fell to as low as 115,000 kronor in 1923.

As of 1953 the Foundation has had much more freedom in deciding how to invest its money, and return on the investments has risen to affect the amount of the award.

In 1993 the Nobel Prize was worth 6,700,000 kronor (about $800,000).

The Nobel Foundation's net worth in the same year was 1,783,000,000,000 kronor.

How are the laureates chosen?

Some practical problems arose at once when it came to determining the authority of those making the awards. Regulations had to be written, since the will was expressed in such general terms that it was vague in several respects.

Invitation to Professor A. Gullstrand to propose a candidate for the Nobel Prize for Chemistry, 1908.

The phrase "during the preceding year" could not be followed literally since years of research lie behind the work of a prizewinner.

Not anyone may propose a candidate. Each prize has its rules for who may make proposals — such as academies, professors, former laureates, and certain institutions.

From these suggested names, the Nobel Committees pick a number of candidates. They then present their proposals to the prize-awarding bodies. The number of names proposed is increasing all the time. Nowadays about 200 candidates are suggested for the science prizes and about 100 for the prizes for peace and literature.

The proposals must be sent in by February 1st at the latest. Once they have arrived, an intense screening process begins which leads to one or more persons being awarded that year's prize. In physics, chemistry, and medicine the prize is shared increasingly often. This is a natural development, since most research is done by teams and not by a lone genius. However, the prize may not be shared by more than three persons at a time. Only individuals may be awarded a Nobel Prize. The exception is the Peace Prize, which can also be awarded to an institution.

In his will, Alfred Nobel designated five subject areas from which laureates would be chosen. Today there is a sixth prize, "The Prize in Economic Sciences in Memory of Alfred Nobel", which has been awarded since 1969. The amount, equal to that of the other prizes, is donated by the Bank of Sweden. The laureate receives his award together with the other prizewinners at the Solemn Festival of the Nobel Foundation in Stockholm's Concert House.

The prize-awarding ceremony

The Nobel festivities on December 10th are celebrated in two cities. The Peace Prize is awarded at a formal ceremony in the Oslo City Hall by the Chairperson of the Norwegian Nobel Committee. Other prizes are awarded in the Stockholm Concert House, which seats at most 1,800 guests.

Before a formally dressed audience and millions of television viewers, the laureates receive their awards consisting of a check, a diploma, and a gold medal with the picture of the donor.

The participation of Swedish Royalty is also an important feature of the stately festival atmosphere that frames the Nobel festivities. The first time the prizes were awarded, in 1901, King Oscar II was traveling and Crown Prince Gustaf presented the awards in his place.

Today a demanding audience of up to a billion people around the world can follow the magnificent drama on television.

We can sit comfortably in our living rooms and see both the prize-awarding ceremony and the banquet.

"Court" reporters provide a lively description of the laureates and the royalty present, with details of their families, their orders and medals, and their jewelry.

The King of Sweden still hands the prize to the proud laureates in person.

The obverse side of the Nobel Medals for Physics, Chemistry, Medicine, and Literature.

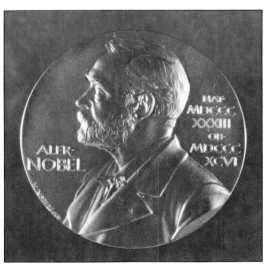

© The Nobel Foundation.

NOBELSTIFTELSENS HÖGTIDSDAG

Torsdagen den 10 december 1992 kl. 16.30
i Konserthusets stora sal

PROGRAM

"Kungssången"

"Rákóczy Marsch" ur Fausts fördömelse . . . . Hector Berlioz

Pristagarna intar sina platser på estraden

Hälsningstal av professor Lars Gyllensten, ordförande i Nobelstiftelsens styrelse

Symfoni nr 8 F-dur op. 93, sats 3
. . . . Ludwig van Beethoven

Överlämnande av 1992 års Nobelpris i fysik till *Georges Charpak* efter presentationstal av professor Carl Nordling

Överlämnande av 1992 år Nobelpris i kemi till *Rudolph A. Marcus* efter presentationstal av professor Lennart Eberson

"Jungfrun under lind". Solist Gösta Winbergh
. . . . Wilhelm Peterson-Berger

Överlämnande av 1992 års Nobelpris i fysiologi eller medicin till *Edmond H. Fischer* och *Edwin G. Krebs* efter presentationstal av professor Hans Jörnvall

"Una furtiva lagrima" ur Kärleksdrycken. Solist Gösta Winbergh
. . . . Gaetano Donizetti

Överlämnande av 1992 års Nobelpris i litteratur till *Derek Walcott* efter presentationstal av professor Kjell Espmark

"Tidens rytm" ur Orfeus i sta'n . . . . Hilding Rosenberg

Överlämnande av Sveriges Riksbanks pris i ekonomisk vetenskap till Alfred Nobels Minne för 1992 till *Gary S. Becker* efter presentationstal av professor Assar Lindbeck

"Du gamla, Du fria"

"Drottningens av Saba festmarsch"
ur Den förlorade sonen. . . . . Hugo Alfvén
Spelas medan gästerna lämnar salen

Musiken utföres av
Kungliga Filharmoniska Orkestern i Stockholm
Solist: Gösta Winbergh, tenor
Dirigent: Niklas Willén

———

Blommorna är en gåva från
Azienda di Promozione Turistica di Sanremo

*Thursday, December 10 th, 1992 at 4.30 p.m.
in the Grand Auditorium of the Concert Hall*

PROGRAMME

"Kungssången"

"Rákóczy March" from Damnation of Faust. . . . . Hector Berlioz

The Laureates take their seats on the stage

Speech by Professor Lars Gyllensten, Chairman of the Board of the Nobel
Foundation

3rd movement from Symphony No. 8 F major op. 93
. . . . Ludwig van Beethoven

Presentation of the Nobel Prize in Physics 1992 to *Georges Charpak* after
a speech by Professor Carl Nordling

Presentation of the Nobel Prize in Chemistry 1992 to *Rudolf A. Marcus*
after a speech by Professor Lennart Eberson

"The Maiden under the Lime Tree". Soloist Gösta Winbergh
. . . . Wilhelm Peterson-Berger

Presentation of the Nobel Prize in Physiology or Medicine 1992 to
Edmond H. Fischer and *Edwin G. Krebs* after a speech by Professor Hans
Jörnvall

"Una furtiva lagrima" from L'elisir d'amore. Soloist Gösta Winbergh
. . . . Gaetano Donizetti

Presentation of the Nobel Prize in Literature 1992 to *Derek Walcott* after a
speech by Professor Kjell Espmark

"Rythm of Time" ´from Orpheus in Town. . . . . . . Hilding Rosenberg

Presentation of the Sveriges Riksbank (Bank of Sweden) Prize in
Economic Sciences in Memory of Alfred Nobel 1992 to *Gary S. Becker*
after a speech by Professor Assar Lindbeck

The Swedish national anthem "Du gamla, du fria"

"Festivity March" from The Prodigal Son. . . . . Hugo Alfvén
Played while the guests are leaving the auditorium

Music performed by
The Royal Stockholm Philharmonic Orchestra
Soloist: Gösta Winbergh, tenor
Conductor:: Niklas Willén

———

The flowers are graciously provided by
Azienda di Promozione Turistica di Sanremo

The Nobel Banquet

Kung Carl XVI Gustaf is the guest of honor at the Nobel Banquet.

The Nobel Banquet

For many, the Nobel Banquet is the climax of the Nobel festivities. From the Stockholm Concert House, where the prizes are awarded, the guests move to the Stockholm City Hall, with the three crowns symbol on its tower.

The City Hall is beautifully situated by Lake Mälar, where the water licks its foundation stones. Inside the building, one is fascinated by the austere interior which has seen so much pomp and circumstance.

For a few hours the world's mass media follow every event

The Nobel Banquet in the Blue Hall.

in the great banquet hall, which is called the Blue Hall. It is an enormous arrangement and everything must work perfectly, down to the last detail. The preparations are carried out meticulously.

The total cost of Nobel Week in Stockholm and Oslo in 1992 amounted to 4,600,000 kronor.

The guests and staff

You cannot "sneak in" to the Nobel Banquet. The number of invitations has been set at 1,288. There is a place card for every person and everyone must show an invitation at the door.

Who is invited to the banquet?
    The Nobel Foundation has had to set up a number of strict criteria for the invitations. Top priority goes to international guests — primarily those who represent science and literature.

Serving the food at the Nobel Banquet is precision work.

There are two ways by which a Swedish citizen can obtain one of the desirable seats at the tables. One way is to be among those involved in the preparations for the Nobel festivities. The other is to be a donor to, or supporter of, science.

Of the 1,288 guests, 88 are placed at the long head table and 250 are university and college students. Students are, after all, the Nobel laureates of tomorrow.

In order for a student to be invited to the banquet, no special area of study is required: they are selected by lottery. If a student is interested, he or she must apply at his or her college.

There are persons other than the banquet guests who will also need food and drink. They are the security officers, bodyguards, selected journalists and certain embassy staff who do not sit at the tables in the Blue Hall, but eat behind the grand staircase and in the City Hall Restaurant.

The tables are completely set before the banquet — a procedure that takes about five hours per 20 places. The distance between the tables is measured and also between the dishes, so that everything will come out even.

Serving so many guests requires meticulous planning. All movements the serving staff will have to make are measured and timed.

It must be known down to the second how long it will take to walk down the grand stairway from the Golden Hall, all the way to each table. For the great ice-cream procession, it takes three minutes from the moment at which the waiters appear in the doorway with their trays until the last of their long line reaches his or her table. The serving of other dishes takes about two minutes.

A large staff is needed to ensure that everything moves smoothly and satisfactorily. In addition to the restaurant general manager, banquet hall manager, banquet hall assistant, and head chef, the following are needed:

8 headwaiters
210 waiters and waitresses
20 chefs
20 maintenance staff (dishwashers, distribution, etc.)
5 wine stewards

Duty at the Nobel Banquet is a much sought-after job. Many of the same people help out year after year. One man, for example, travels all the way from Hungary every year to work in the kitchen! Whoever wants to work at the banquet should be in good physical condition: serving staff have to walk about five kilometers (3 miles) during the evening. Just to be safe, there is always reserve staff ready to take over if someone should become ill or not meet the standard required. It sometimes happens that someone may be taken off duty in the middle of the banquet if he or she cannot handle his or her duties or becomes too nervous.

How do you get taken on staff for the Noble Banquet?

Often you know someone who is already working there. But there are also many who write or get in touch with the City Hall Restaurant, and if they have good references they may have a chance.

If the Restaurant is not sure of you or your skills, you may be allowed to come and work there for a while at another banquet. But those interested should get their applications in by September.

Food and drink

Planning the menu for a Nobel Banquet is really like passing through the eye of the needle. Many experts from around the world will have an opinion and will want to give advice. Three proposed menus are produced every year by the head chef,

The food stops in the Golden Hall on its way from the kitchen to the Blue Hall.

chef, and general manager of the City Hall Restaurant. The members of the Nobel Foundation then present their opinions on the dishes and composition of the menu at a test dinner.

Some foods, such as shellfish, are avoided since they may aggravate allergies. Other points to be considered are the fact that the guests come from many different cultures, that the food should have a Scandinavian touch, and that it should be varied. It should also be suitable from the point of view of cooking and warming. The kitchen is four stories above the Golden Hall, where the food stops on its way to the guests in the Blue Hall, yet another story below. In order for the food to be heated up perfectly, exact information is required on how long each speaker will speak. If someone speaks 5-10 minutes longer than planned, the food will not be of the same quality.

To illustrate what and how much is served, the following is a report from the 1992 Nobel Banquet.

1,288 guests enjoyed:

Grouse patties with herb sauce and Nobel croissants.
Lake Vättern char in juniper marinade with buttered asparagus, dill cream and rice.
Nobel ice-cream parfait with spun sugar and petits fours.
For the first course: 500 grouse; 320 bottles of Moet & Chandon Brut Imperial.
For the main course: 400 kg of Lake Vättern char, 14 liters of dill cream, 100 kg of asparagus; 330 bottles of 1988 Chateau de Cruzeau.
For the dessert: 140 ice-cream parfaits; 160 bottles of Grådask Very Superior Old Port.
After dinner 270 liters of coffee was served.
There was also a bottle of Ramlösa mineral water at each of the 1,288 places.
The table setting involved 450 meters of linen tablecloth, 2,576 silver knives, 3,864 silver forks, 1,288 silver spoons, 5,152 glasses, 5,152 dishes, and 1,288 coffee cups and saucers.
The tables were decorated with 4,200 red carnations and 8 kg of mimosa donated by the mayor of San Remo.

Other groups also like to celebrate at the City Hall with the same menu as the one at the Nobel Banquet. The special Nobel porcelain and cutlery, however, are used only for the Nobel festivities.

Remarkably, no serious accidents have occurred depite the great number of people and the extreme pressure and massive supervision the staff are subjected to. Journalists and TV producers would just love to see a piece of ice cream slide down the front of a low-cut ball gown.

On one occasion the toastmaster fainted from the heat, but that was the only accident the Nobel Banquet has noted.

NOBELPRISET

The Nobel Prize

■

NOBELSTIFTELSENS HÖGTIDSDAG

DEN 10 DECEMBER

1992

PRISUTDELNING

I

KONSERTHUSET

PROGRAMME

6.45 p.m.	Guests are requested to take their seats in the Blue Hall
6.45 p.m.	Students bearing the standards of the Stockholm student unions parade through the Blue Hall to music performed by students from the Stockholm College of Music
7.00 p.m.	The guests of honour enter in procession to the music of "Fanfare" by Jacques Nicolas Lemmens
7.05 p.m.	His Majesty's toast is proposed by Professor Lars Gyllensten, Chairman of the Board of the Nobel Foundation
7.07 p.m.	A toast to Alfred Nobel's memory is proposed by H.M. the King

The serving of each of the three Banquet courses is preceded by a procession

The garlands of pine branches and floral decorations in white and yellow from the Prize Award Cermony in the Concert Hall recur in the first two processions, presented by female and male dancers and singers

The third procession, which precedes the dessert, includes a solo dance performance to choreography inspired by Loïe Fuller, a choreographer who worked in Paris at the turn of the century

Choreographed and directed by Professor Margaretha Åsberg, National College of Dance

Soloist: Anja Birnbaum, The Pyramids Dance Group
Organ music: Anders Bondeman, organist, S:t Jacob Church, Stockholm
Dancers from the National College of Dance, and the Romeo and Juliet
Choir of the Royal Dramatic Theatre
Costumes: Ulrika Wedin
Lighting: Torkel Blomkvist

Speeches by Laureates

The Stockholm Academic Male Choir together with Gösta Winbergh, Royal Court Singer, under the direction of Göte Widlund, conductor

10.00 p.m.	The Royal Family receives the Laureates in the Prince's Gallery
10.00 p.m.	Dancing to "The Kustbandet Orchestra", playing hot and swing
11.00 p.m.	Dancing to "Hot Pans" Steelband, playing calypso and soca
11.30 p.m. – midnight	Dancing to "The Kustbandet Orchestra" continued

Other Participants:

Ensemble from the Stockholm College of Music
Jan Hartman, master of ceremonies
Mats Ericson, City Hall organist
Olle Hermansen och Stig Rydqvist, fanfar trumpeters
The Kustbandet Orchestra
"Hot Pans" Steelband

*The concept team behind the design of the dinnerware and table
linen set and the processions*

Ove Thorsén, Artist and Director of Studies, Department of Design and
Crafts, Gothenburg, University
Åke Livstedt, M.A.
Magnus Silverhielm, Architect SAR

*The flowers are graciously provided by
Azienda di Promozione Turistica di Sanremo.*

MENU

TERRINE DE SAUMON ET DE SOLE À L'ANETH
SAUCE AUX OEUFS D'ABLETTE

FILET EXTÉRIEUR D'AGNEAU RÔTI, CHAMPIGNONS DE SAISON
CAROTTES ET SALSIFIS NOIRS GLACÉS AU MIEL
SAUCE AU CIDRE

GLACE NOBEL AU CHOCOLAT BLANC
ET À LA GROSEILLE ROUGE

———

VINS

MOËT & CHANDON
Brut Impérial
1984 CHÂTEAU MOUTON BARONNE PHILIPPE
Cru Classé – Sélection Nobel
1983 JOHANNISBERG BOTRYTIS RIESLING,

———

EAU MINERALE DE RAMLÖSA

———

CAFÉ

———

BUFFET

ABSOLUT VODKA
HENNESSY V.S.O.P. Privilège
PETITE LIQUEUR par Moët & Chandon
JOHNNIE WALKER RED & BLACK LABEL
BACARDI RUM
GORDON'S GIN
CAMPARI
BOISSONS DE PRIPPS

Floral decorations

Luxuriant floral decorations always form part of the Nobel festivities. Thousands of flowers are served up in a variety of settings, which television unfortunately cannot quite portray in all their glory.

The town of San Remo donates all the flowers for both the prize-awarding ceremony in the Concert House and the banquet in the City Hall. There are two reasons for this. In the first place, Alfred Nobel lived in the northern Italian town at the end of his life. And, of course, the floral arrangement has great public relations value and San Remo is the cut flower capital of the Riviera.

The flowers are shipped from Italy either by air or in specially cooled trucks to the Italian tourist office in Stockholm. In Sweden Hässelby Flowers has the responsibility of arranging and distributing the flowers tastefully and aesthetically.

The lighting is very important if all the flower-bedecked pillars and aisles are to appear at their best.

After the prize-awarding ceremony in the Concert Hall, all the flowers are given to the student union which collects them the same evening and takes them to a late-night student celebration.

Where the laureates stay

The honor of hosting the Nobel guests has been granted to Stockholm's Grand Hotel ever since 1901. In the first years the Nobel Banquet was also held in the hotel's Hall of Mirrors, but it was later moved to the City Hall because more space was needed. The Noble Foundation pays the bill for the laureate and his or her spouse. If the couple has young children, they are also included. Otherwise friends and relatives must pay their own hotel bill.

Sometimes a prizewinner brings a very large group of supporters, who may have to stay at other hotels. The Nobel laureates in literature are often accompanied by a large group.

The prizewinners' time in Stockholm is extremely limited and fully booked. Nevertheless, a few of them have managed to leave a lasting memory with the Grand Hotel's staff and other guests.

Grand Hotel - The Nobel Hotel.

The 1968 laureate in literature, Wole Soyinka from Nigeria, was a great personality whose charm enchanted everyone. He even led singing and jazz evenings in the hotel bar!

Professor George Hitchings from the United States, a 1988 prizewinner in medicine, arrived in Stockholm newly in love with a woman who was much younger than he. During his stay at the Grand Hotel, he caught sight of the hotel's china which carried the initials G.H. He was so delighted that his initials and the hotel's were the same that he later wanted to buy a set of the china for his new home when he married.

A 1988 laureate in physics, Melvin Schwarz from the United States, had a daughter who was working at a Hilton hotel in California. She came with her father to Stockholm for the Nobel ceremony and was so taken with the Grand Hotel that she wanted to work there. As a result, she was employed there for two years, including 1991 when all former laureates were invited to special 90th anniversary Nobel festivities. It was the first time a Nobel laureate staying at the hotel had a child there as an employee.

Once an Asian prizewinner awoke in fright when a traditional Swedish Lucia, with burning candles on her head, appeared in the bedroom with her maids one gray morning in December. The Lucia procession is an old tradition, but nowadays the guests are warned in advance.

Odds and Ends

For most people, receiving a Nobel Prize once is the dream of a lifetime. Receiving it twice is almost Utopia.

But despite the razor-sharp competition, a few people have actually succeeded in being awarded two Nobel Prizes.

Linus Pauling, USA, is alone in having received the prize twice without having shared it: for Chemistry in 1954 and for Peace in 1962 (for his efforts in opposing nuclear weapons).

John Bardeen, USA, has shared the Physics Prize twice: in 1956 and 1972.

Fredrik Sanger, Britain, was awarded the Chemistry Prize twice, alone in 1958 and shared in 1980.

Marie Curie shared the 1903 Physics Prize with her husband Pierre and Henri Becquerel. In 1911 she won the Chemistry Prize alone.

Marie Curie shared the 1903 Physics Prize with her husband, Pierre Curie.

Marie Curie's daughter Irène Joliot was awarded the 1953 Chemistry Prize.

Others who have followed in their parents' footsteps have been Aage Bohr, Denmark, who was born in 1922, the same year in which his father won the Physics Prize. The son received his Physics Prize in 1975.

Kai Siegbahn, Sweden, won the 1981 Physics Prize. His father, Manne Siegbahn, had received the same prize in 1924.

The von Euler family, Sweden, had the same relationship: the father, Hans, received the Chemistry Prize in 1929 and the son, Ulf, won the Medicine Prize in 1970.

Bertha von Suttner, Austria, received the 1905 Nobel Prize for Peace. For a brief time she was employed by Alfred Nobel as his private secretary and he fell in love with her.

Two Swedes were awarded the prize posthumously: Erik Axel Karlfeldt for Literature in 1931 and Dag Hammarskjöld for Peace in 1961.

Jean-Paul Sartre, France, declined to accept the Literature Prize in 1964.

Alexander Solzhenitsyn, Soviet Union, was awarded the 1970 Literature Prize but could not accept it because he would have been refused re-entry into the Soviet Union if he did so. But in 1974 he was able to attend the prize-awarding ceremony in Stockholm and he received his prize at that time.

Adolf Hitler did not receive a prize, but he forbade German citizens to accept any Nobel Prize after the German peace activist and pacifist Carl von Ossietzky was awarded the Peace Prize in 1935.

Hjalmar Branting, Sweden, considered that Alfred Nobel's idea for giving prizes of money was "capitalistic razzle-dazzle". He won the Peace Prize himself in 1921.

Five Nobel laureates. Left to right: Svedberg, Fleming, Tiselius, Chain and Theorell.

44

THE NOBEL PRIZE IN PHYSICS

Wilhelm Röntgen 1845-1923

We have all heard Röntgen's name, but we may not know so much about the man behind it.

He was born on March 27th 1845 in Lennep, Germany, the son of a carpenter. In his youth he studied in different places in Europe and later became a professor at no fewer than four universities.

In 1895, at the advanced age (for a researcher) of 50, Röntgen became interested in studying cathode rays and suddenly discovered a new, previously unknown type of ray. He was so enthusiastic that he slept and ate in his laboratory.

The new rays had the ability to pass through different materials and they also affected photographic plates. Röntgen had discovered what he called "X-rays" - in some languages called "Röntgen rays" - a medium for seeing and photographing the innards of the body. There was enormous excitement when Röntgen published his photographs, and he immediately became the favorite of learned academies and educational institutions throughout the world. The Kaiser of Germany himself elevated his commoner subject to the nobility.

Wilhelm von Röntgen continued to study and carry out further research on the use and properties of X-rays. Few discoveries have had such universal significance as X-rays - mainly in medicine but also in science and technology.

In 1901, the first year of the Nobel Prizes, Wilhelm Röntgen received the Physics Prize "in recognition of the extraordinary services he has rendered by the discovery of the remarkable rays subsequently named after him."

Albert Einstein 1879-1955

"It doesn't matter, he'll never succeed in anything," said the school principal to young Albert Einstein's father when asked what vocation the boy should choose.

Albert Einstein was born in Germany in 1879, of Jewish parents. In childhood he seemed almost backward, and by the age of nine he could still not speak clearly. The family moved to Switzerland where Albert became a citizen in 1901. His former lack of interest in schoolwork changed to a great enthusiasm for his studies.

In 1914 he was appointed head of the Kaiser Wilhelm Institute of Physics in Berlin. The government created a special position for him so that he could do research and devote himself to science without having to think about lecturing or other extraneous duties.

However, Einstein viewed what was happening in the Germany of the thirties with anxiety. Since he was Jewish not even his special position as a successful scientist could protect him, and in 1933 the Nazi government fired him from his post. He emigrated to the United States the same year.

He became a citizen of his new country and stayed there the rest of his life. On the outbreak of war in 1939, Einstein warned President Roosevelt that Germany had the capacity to use atomic power for military purposes. In this way he contributed to the fact that the United States accelerated its own effort to develop an atomic bomb. Later he led the movement to put this terrible weapon under the control of the United Nations.

The famous "theory of relativity" was formulated in 1905 and published in its entirety in 1915-16, giving Einstein a worldwide reputation. It became popular through the interpretation that "everything is relative", and thus all opinions are equally valid - an idea of which Einstein himself disapproved.

In his search for basic laws of the universe, he proposed the pioneering formula that described the sum of all energy in the universe as a constant.

Albert Einstein was awarded the 1921 Nobel Prize for Physics for "his services to Theoretical Physics, and especially for his discovery of the law of photoelectric effect".

In his old age the great physicist was made a most remarkable and flattering offer. In 1952 he was invited to become the President of Israel. He declined, saying that he did not have a head for human problems.

Niels Bohr 1885-1962

Niels Bohr was born in Copenhagen. He studied natural sciences at Copenhagen University where, at the age of 22, he received the Gold Medal of the Danish Scientific Society for his determination of the surface tension of water.

In 1911-12 he worked at Cambridge under J. J. Thomson and, not least, in Manchester under the great chemist Rutherford. This period gave Bohr considerable stimulation for future research.

In 1913, at the age of 27, he developed the modern picture of the atom by combining Rutherford's model and Planck's "quantum". He created a functioning model of the atom to explain the spectrum of water and the structure of the periodic table.

With his droplet model of 1936 Bohr made an important contribution to the understanding of fission. Niels Bohr is one of the founders of 20th century physics. He used to tell his students, "You should consider every sentence that I utter not a statement but a question".

Denmark was occupied by Germany in the Second World War and Niels Bohr fled to Sweden under dramatic circumstances in the autumn of 1943. He was warned that the Gestapo were coming to his home to take him to Germany where his knowledge would be useful to the Nazis. Bohr managed to escape to Sweden on a boat across the Sound, taking his notes with him, including the main formulas for future atomic research. From Sweden he continued to the United States where he eagerly took part in the work on the atomic bomb in 1943-45. In 1922 Niels Bohr was awarded the Nobel Prize for Physics for "his services in the investigation of the structure of atoms and of the radiation emanating from them".

THE NOBEL PRIZE
IN CHEMISTRY

Lord Rutherford 1871-1937

Ernest Rutherford was born in New Zealand in 1871, but soon the whole world was his workplace. He was appointed Professor of Physics at McGill University in Montreal in 1898 and came to Manchester in 1907, Cambridge in 1919, and London in 1920. He became Sir Ernest Rutherford in 1914 and was created Baron Rutherford of Nelson in 1931.

He was awarded the Nobel Prize at the age of 37 — one of the youngest laureates ever.

What was it that this man did to give him such success and fame?

His first studies of magnetism led to the invention of a magnetic detector for electrical waves. Then he devoted himself to the problems and properties of radioactivity and radiation. Among other things he discovered alpha and beta radiation, and identified alpha particles and helium nuclei.

When Rutherford fired alpha particles at atoms of the lighter basic elements, he found that the nucleus of a nitrogen atom could be split. In this way he showed that protons are included in the nuclei.

In 1908 Lord Rutherford received the Nobel Prize for Chemistry for "his investigations into the disintegration of the elements, and the chemistry of radioactive substances".

Marie Curie 1867-1934

"The most brilliant woman born in Europe" was one of many comments referring to the tenacious, strong-willed Marie Curie.

She was born in Poland in 1867 as Mania Sklodowska. It is said that when she was four years old and her family had gathered to hear a reading, she took the book during a pause and amazed everyone by continuing the reading.

In 1891 she went to study at the Sorbonne in Paris, and at the same time changed her name to Marie. There she met her future husband, the physicist Pierre Curie, whom she married in 1895.

In a primitive little laboratory the couple discovered a new basic element: radium. In 1903 they shared with Henri Becquerel the Nobel Prize for Physics, for their basic research into radioactivity. Only a couple of years later, Pierre Curie died.

However Marie continued her research. In 1911 her work resulted in yet another Nobel Prize, this time for chemistry, "in recognition of her services to the advancement of chemistry by the discovery of the elements radium and polonium, by the isolation of radium and the study of the nature and compounds of this remarkable element.".

In 1914, when the First World War broke out, Marie Curie went to the front as a volunteer, despite great opposition from the French government. There she helped out with the newly fashionable X-rays.

She also loaned her prize money of 140,000 kronor to the French nation. The money was accepted with joy but she never got it back again. In 1934 Marie Curie died of leukemia, after having worked unprotected for years with radioactive substances. The natural force which she herself had discovered now claimed its due.

Linus Pauling 1901-

The American chemist and pacifist Linus Pauling is the only person to have won two non-shared Nobel Prizes.

Pauling was appointed to the position of professor at the California Institute of Technology in 1931. He began his career by studying the structure of crystals and molecules. In the 1930s and 40s he worked with quantum mechanics, studying the forces that bind atoms in a molecule - work which has given inspiration to generations of chemists.

Working on models for the structure of proteins, he was awarded the Nobel Prize for Chemistry in 1954 "for his research into the nature of the chemical bond and its application to the elucidation of the structure of complex substances".

As a result of the terrible lesson taught by the atomic bombs at the end of the Second World War, Pauling became a member of the Emergency Committee of Atomic Scientists, led by Albert Einstein. Because of the position he took, he was subjected to harassment during the McCarthy era, and his passport was taken from him.

In 1958 Pauling presented a petition to the United Nations signed by more than 11,000 scientists from around the world, urging an end to nuclear weapons tests. The same year he published "No More Wars!" which attracted great attention.

In 1963 Linus Pauling was awarded the 1962 Nobel Peace Prize for his efforts in resisting atomic weapons. The same day, December 10th 1963, the announcement came that the ban on nuclear weapons testing had been signed by the Soviet Union, the United Kingdom, and the United States.

THE NOBEL PRIZE IN
PHYSIOLOGY OR MEDICINE

Ivan Pavlov 1849-1936

Ivan Petrovitch Pavlov was a Russian physician and physiologist. After attending the Academy of Military Medicine in St. Petersburg and studying experimental physiology for two years in Germany, Pavlov was appointed to a professorship in the Siberian city of Tomsk in 1890.

His "exile" to Siberia was short-lived, however, and Pavlov soon returned to the capital, St. Petersburg, where he was given large resources for his work. Using dogs in his experiments, he studied the relationship of the nervous system to the physiology of the organs of digestion. Pavlov showed that the secretion of the gastric juices, and thus the digestion of food, was affected by mental attitudes and impulses.

Sooner or later every schoolchild hears about "Pavlov's dogs" and the concept of "conditioned reflexes" - that is, similar repeated stimuli can cause similar bodily reactions.

Pavlov's discoveries became very important for the psychology of learning.

IVAN PETROVITCH PAVLOV

In 1904 Ivan Pavlov was awarded the Nobel Prize for Physiology or Medicine "in recognition of his work on the physiology of digestion, through which knowledge on vital aspects of the subject has been transformed and enlarged".

Sir Alexander Fleming 1881-1955

Alexander Fleming was born on August 16th 1881, on Lochfield Farm, Scotland. He grew up under very poor conditions, and his mother was widowed with eight children to care for.

He was educated at the Kilmarnock Academy and the St. Mary's Hospital Medical School at London University. After graduating, he worked at St. Mary's Hospital under the famous Almroth Wright, a pioneer in vaccine therapy.

In 1928 an event occurred which many considered a stroke of luck. The contents of a dish that had been forgotten in the laboratory, staphylococcus bacteria, had become contaminated by mould.

Fleming noticed that the mould killed the original bacteria. This was enough to awaken his interest and a desire to do further research. Together with Howard Florey and Boris Chain he continued to refine and perfect his discoveries.

It took many more years before the discovery that the mould produced substances that killed bacteria could lead to the practical use of penicillin.

In 1941 it was tried on a human being for the first time. A policeman lay dying of blood poisoning. He was given penicillin and gradually began to improve. But there was not enough penicillin, the policeman grew worse, and later died. That was the beginning of the "wonder drug" which has helped and even saved the lives of millions of people throughout the world.

In 1944 he was awarded a knighthood and the following year Sir Alexander Fleming shared the Nobel Prize for Physiology or Medicine with his co-researchers Florey and Chain for "the discovery of penicillin and its curative effect in various infectious diseases".

Konrad Lorentz 1903-1989

Konrad Lorentz of Austria studied the behavior of animals when he was a child, and later studied medicine, zoology and psychology. In 1939 he was appointed Professor of Psychology at Königsberg University.

His research was interrupted by the dark shadow of the Second World War. Lorentz became a physician in the German army and later was taken prisoner of war in the Soviet Union.

In 1948 Lorentz returned to Austria to continue his studies of animal behavior. Above all he studied the instinctive behavior of birds, and did pioneering work on the "imprinting" of newborn ducks. Lorentz laid the foundation for the science of ethology (the study of animal behavior). He also studied human behavior and was especially interested in the study of aggression.

According to Lorentz, both animals and humans have four major driving forces in their behavior: hunger, love, flight, and aggression.

Lorentz' publications include "Animal and Human" 1935, "In Conversation with Animals" 1949, and "Aggression" 1966.

In 1973 Konrad Lorentz shared the Nobel Prize for Physiology or Medicine with Karl von Frisch and Niko Tinbergen "for their discoveries concerning organization and elicitation of individual and social behavior patterns".

THE NOBEL PRIZE
IN LITERATURE

George Bernard Shaw 1856-1950

Shaw was born in Dublin, the son of an alcoholic, protestant, unsuccessful merchant. "My father taught me to swim, but nothing else," Shaw once stated.

He came to London in his twenties and lived in poverty, supporting himself with difficulty by writing newspaper articles. He joined the socialist and pacifist Fabian Society. After a number of unsuccessful novels he wrote his first play of social criticism in 1892, "Widowers' Houses". Even more challenging was "Mrs. Warren's Profession" in which marriage was equated with prostitution.

Shaw soon won world recognition as a dramatist, even though his debut had come as late as the age of 39. His most famous play is "Pygmalion", in which Prof. Higgens teaches the flower girl Eliza to speak upper-class English. His screen version of the play won an Academy Award and became even more famous in the 1950s when adapted as the musical, "My Fair Lady".

Shaw was also a prominent music and drama critic, with a crushing and humorous style.

His targets were prejudice and superstition, and he argued on behalf of many unpopular ideas: teetotalism, vegetarianism, pacifism, anti-nicotinism, and socialism. With such ideas, and especially his way of promoting them, Shaw was constantly in trouble. Eventually he became an institution: a brilliant, original cultural personality.

George Bernard Shaw was awarded the 1925 Nobel Prize for Literature "for his work which is marked by both idealism and humanity. its stimulating satire often being infused with a singular poetic beauty".

At first he refused the prize, but later changed his mind and donated the prize money to a foundation for promoting Swedish literature in English.

Sir Winston Churchill 1874-1965

To most people, Winston Churchill is synonymous with the Second World War, a fat cigar, and the eternal V-sign. Churchill was the symbol - indeed, the primal force - that refused against all odds to give in to Nazi barbarism.

With his strong personality, eloquence, and ability to instill courage, he was one of the reasons that Great Britain could survive the bombings and blockades to become victorious in the end. Churchill's name will always be engraved in the British national soul.

Winston Churchill was born on November 30th 1874 at Blenheim Palace. His upbringing followed the traditional program for a person of the upper classes in Victorian England. For him, that meant a strict education at private schools where he was unhappy right from the beginning, and where he was considered a failure.

The young Winston Churchill's future seemed very uncertain when he finally came to the cavalry. The reason that he was accepted there was that he could afford to keep his own horse.

He was looking for honor and repute, and soon he would find both.

Photo from the University Library, Uppsala

Churchill was drawn to danger and adventure. India, Cuba, Sudan and South Africa were various scenes of war to which he came as a soldier but where he often took his first literary steps as a war correspondent.

Churchill's reports from the front attracted attention and opened the door to a career in politics.

He wrote his first book in 1898, "The Story of the Malakand Field Force".

Once in the maelstrom of politics, titles and appointments rapidly appeared for the sometimes rough-hewn and difficult politician. A number of cabinet positions eventually resulted in his leading the country as Prime Minister during the war years.

As a public speaker, Churchill was magnificent. Many of his speeches became classics. On July 4th 1940, when the evacuation of Dunkerque was being completed, he said the following:

"Even though large tracts of Europe and many old and famous states have fallen or may fall into the grip of the Gestapo and all the odious apparatus of Nazi rule, we shall not flag or fail. We shall go on to the end. We shall fight in France, we shall fight on the seas and the oceans, we shall fight with growing confidence and growing strength in the air, we shall defend our island, whatever the cost may be. We shall fight on the beaches, we shall fight on the landing grounds, we shall fight in the fields and in the streets, we shall fight in the hills; we shall never surrender.

"And even if, which I do not for a moment believe, this island or a large part of it were subjugated and starving, then our Empire beyond the seas, armed and guarded by the British Fleet, would carry on the struggle, until, in God's good time, the New World, with all its power and might, steps forth to the rescue and the liberation of the Old."

To a great extent Churchill's political career overshadowed

his literary talent. But here too he was brilliant. Few have mastered the English language to such perfection. What is surprising is how this man had time to be so prolific in his literary achievement when his political career represented more than a life's work.

Churchill's publications include a biography of his father, "Lord Randolph Churchill I-II", "The World Crises I-V", "My Early life", "Marlborough, His Life and Times I-V", and "The Second World War I-VI".

In 1953 Sir Winston Churchill received the Nobel Prize for Literature "for his mastery of historical and biographical description as well as for brilliant oratory in defending exalted human values".

Silhouette from the University Library, Uppsala.

Ernest Hemingway 1899-1961

The myth and the legend. Who was he?

Sometimes reality surpasses fiction, and in the case of Ernest Hemingway his whole life was a novel. He was born in Oak Park, Illinois on July 21st 1899. He came to Europe as a volunteer in the American Ambulance Corps in the First World War. He remained in Europe in the 20s and 30s, working as a journalist. During this time he traveled to various countries, gaining a wealth of ideas, suggestions and memories that he later used in his writing.

His literary debut in 1923 came in the form of "Three Stories and Ten Poems". A few years later, in 1926, "The Sun Also Rises" was his breakthrough. Other famous books are "A Farewell to Arms" 1929, "For Whom the Bell Tolls" 1940, and "The Old Man and the Sea" 1952.

His books often feature a typical Hemingway hero who, with a good portion of manliness and courage, fights both external physical enemies and personal torment. Privately, it often seemed that Hemingway was trying to live up to the life of his fictional heroes. Or perhaps his stormy life formed the basis of his characters?

War, bullfights, big game hunting, boxing, and deep-sea fishing were some of the ingredients in Hemingway's life - always with women, alcohol and cats to add flavor.

In 1954 Ernest Hemingway was awarded the Noble Prize for Literature "for his mastery of the art of narrative, most recently demonstrated in The Old Man and the Sea, and for the influence that he has exerted on contemporary style."

On July 2nd 1961 Hemingway, suffering from incurable cancer, shot himself in his home in Ketchum, Idaho.

THE NOBEL PEACE PRIZE

Albert Schweitzer 1875-1965

A genius in two senses, Schweitzer was highly gifted as a scientist and musician, and even more so as a Christian humanist.

Albert Schweitzer was born on January 14th 1875 in Alsace, on the border between Germany and France. He was so tied to these two countries that he alternated between the two languages when he wrote his works.

Schweitzer must be considered one of the greatest universal geniuses ever to have lived. After theological studies and the publication of a pioneering work on Paul and Jesus, he turned to music. As a musicologist he became famous internationally for his monumental work, "Johann Sebastian Bach, the Poet Musician", published in 1905.

Schweitzer was also a skilled and famous organist who gave concerts to sold-out houses throughout Europe. Organ builders considered him one of the foremost experts on European organs at that time.

At the age of 21 Albert Schweitzer made a decision which called for enormous inner strength and conviction. Until the age of 30 he would devote himself to theology, music and philosophy, the subjects he loved, but then he would spend the rest of his life in the service of humanity.

Schweitzer kept his promise. When he was 30 he went back to school to study medicine, especially tropical medicine. European intellectuals criticized him strongly when he announced that he would leave his duties to travel to West Africa and found a jungle hospital.

His critics complained, "The white people of the western countries are your business, not the negroes of West Africa. Others who lack your talents for art and science can go out and work among the Africans."

Schweitzer answered, "Of course they can, but they don't."

Together with his wife, Schweitzer built a hospital at Lambaréné in French Equatorial Africa. He financed the whole project himself.

During the First World War Schweitzer was interned and later taken to France as a prisoner of war. After a few depressing years, the Swedish Archbishop Natan Söderblom invited him to Sweden to lecture on ethics. The appreciation and good will that Schweitzer met in Sweden gave him the strength to return to Africa to rebuild his hospital. For the rest of his life he commuted between the hospital in Africa and Europe, where he made lecture and concert tours. The proceeds went to meet the hospital's expenses.

In 1952 Albert Schweitzer was awarded the Nobel Peace Prize.

Martin Luther King, Jr. 1929-1968

"I have a dream..." King held his famous and oft-quoted speech in 1963, when he dreamed that white and black people could live side by side, and that violence would no longer rule but people would be guided by good sense and respect for all living beings.

Martin Luther King, Jr. was born on January 15th 1929 in Atlanta, Georgia. His father was a Baptist preacher and King Jr. grew up in a home steeped in the Christian faith. His father's life and sermons made a great impression on him.

King was very much affected by the cruel racial segregation of the time, and with his personal involvement and authority he soon became the foremost leader of the new awareness that was appearing then. Through various actions, such as bus boycotts and peaceful demonstrations, King and his civil rights movement opened the eyes of America and the world to the injustices of segregation. Thanks to King's strong personality and his policy of "non-violence", many critical moments when violence was on the point of breaking out were transformed into a victory for humanism.

However, the opposition was determined. There were many cases of violence and beatings, but the civil rights movement did not give up the struggle. Eventually American laws were changed to prohibit segregation.

In 1963 a huge peace march was held in Washington. A special fighting song, "We shall overcome", showed that a new era had dawned. In 1964 Martin Luther King, Jr. was awarded the Nobel Prize for Peace. Four years later, in 1968, he fell victim to a white killer's bullets while he was standing on a motel balcony in Memphis, where he had come to organize a demonstration.

Mother Teresa 1910-

She was born Agnes Gonxha Bojaxhiu in the city of Skopje, of Albanian-Yugoslav parentage. Her father died when she was seven years old, leaving her mother with three children to care for.

Religion was very important to the family, and young Agnes loved to sit in the church library and read. The stories of missionaries among the poor people of India made a strong impression on her. At the age of twelve she felt her first call to become a nun, and six years later she waved goodbye to her family and sailed to India. There, as a nun, she joined the Loreto Sisters, an Irish order which had a mission in India. She taught in its schools and it was at this time she changed her name to Teresa.

In 1948 she again heard the call of God, and left the Loreto Sisters to serve "the poorest of the poor" in the slums of Calcutta. In 1950 Mother Teresa formed the Missionaries of Charity and since then the sisters in their blue and white habits have appeared as ministering angels at different places in the world. They work at children's homes, schools for orphans, leper hospitals, and at the last resting places for the dying who have no homes of their own. The sisters are financed entirely through voluntary donations.

Mother Teresa was awarded the 1979 Peace Prize, which she accepted in the name of the poor. Of herself she said only, "I am the pen in the hand of the Lord".

THE BANK OF SWEDEN PRIZE IN ECONOMIC SCIENCES IN MEMORY OF ALFRED NOBEL

Gunnar Myrdal 1898-1987

Gunnar Myrdal was a political scientist, politician, and one of the world's leading economists.

In a number of books and reports, Myrdal has stood out as one of the great political economists of the 20th century. In 1929 he published "The Political Element in Development of Economic Theory".

In the 1930s Myrdal made a number of significant contributions to the theory of money and economic fluctuation, including "Monetary Equilibrium". He also studied, together with his wife Alva, the question of population and in 1944 published "An American Dilemma", a study of the racial question in the United States which gave him international recognition.

Myrdal also studied the problems of the third world, resulting in "An Asian Drama" 1968.

Gunnar Myrdal was a professor of political economy and international economics at Stockholm University. He was also very active in politics and was Minister of Trade in the Social Democratic government of 1945-47. He was Secretary-General of the UN Economic Commission for Europe from 1945-57.

In 1974 Gunnar Myrdal shared the Bank of Sweden Prize in Economic Sciences in Memory of Alfred Nobel with F. A. von Hayek, for "their pioneering work in the theory of money and economic fluctuations and for their penetrating analysis of the interdependence of economic, social and institutional phenomena".

In 1982 his wife Alva Myrdal was awarded the Nobel Peace Prize.

Friedrich August von Hayek 1899-1992

After this Austrian-British economist and political philosopher graduated in law and social studies in the 1920s, he worked on theoretical economics, publishing among other things "Prices and Production".

During the 1920s his books and articles aroused much lively debate. At the beginning of 1929 he predicted the coming depression, which he claimed was due to the fact that the expansive monetary policy of the United States had extended the boom of the 1920s by two years.

In the 1930s Hayek was a pioneer in monetary policy, criticizing the planned economies of the post-war period. At that time his opinions were very controversial, and his analysis of a free market economy did not win a hearing until the end of the 1970s.

From the mid-1940s Hayek's research was directed increasingly at general social analysis. In his famous book "The Road to Serfdom" (1944) he argued that both a planned economy and the welfare state would lead to a restriction of individual freedom.

Hayek's analysis of the interdependence between economics and institutions has had great interdisciplinary significance. In 1974 he shared the Bank of Sweden Prize in Economic Sciences in Memory of Alfred Nobel for "pioneering work in the theory of money and economic fluctuations and for their penetrating analysis of the interdependence of economic, social and institutional phenomena".

Milton Friedman 1912-

The American economist and statistician Milton Friedman was a professor at Chicago University from 1948-77 and was later active at Stanford University.

In the 1930s he worked on economic statistics on the income and expenses of households. His research has included market policies - where is considered pre-eminent in the "Chicago School" - monetary history and methodology.

Friedman has studied the relationship between monetary value and inflation. He believes that efforts to fight inflation must always be given priority even if they may lead to increased unemployment during a period of transition.

Milton Friedman's best known books include "Capitalism and Freedom" 1926 and "A Monetary History of the United States 1867-1960" 1963.

In 1976 Milton Friedman was awarded the Economics Prize "for his achievements in the fields of consumption analysis, monetary history and theory, and for his demonstration of the complexity of stabilization policy".

The selection of Friedman was harshly criticized in many quarters because he was revealed to be an economic advisor to the military junta of Chile.

Year	Physics	Chemistry
1901	W.C. Röntgen (G)	J.H. Van't Hoff (NL)
1902	H.A. Lorentz (NL) P. Zeeman (NL)	H.E. Fischer (G)
1903	A.H. Becquerel (F) P. Curie (F) M.Curie (F)	S.A. Arrhenius (Swe)
1904	J.W.S. Rayleigh (GB)	W. Ramsey (GB)
1905	P.E.A. Lenard (G)	J.F.W.A. von Baeyer (G)
1906	J.J. Thomson (GB)	H. Moissan (F)
1907	A.A. Michelson (US)	E. Buchner (G)
1908	G. Lippman (F)	E. Rutherford (GB)
1909	G. Marconi (I) C.F. Braun (G)	W. Ostwald (G)
1910	J.D. van der Waals (NL)	O. Wallach (G)
1911	W. Wien (G)	M. Curie (F)
1912	N.G. Dalén (Swe)	V. Grignard (F) P. Sabatier (F)
1913	H. Kamerlingh-Onnes (NL)	A. Werner (Swi)
1914	M. von Laue (G)	T.W. Richards (US)
1915	W.H. Bragg (GB) W. L. Bragg (GB)	R.M. Willstätter (G)
1916	Not awarded	Not awarded
1917	C.G. Barkla (GB)	Not awarded
1918	M.K.E.L. Planck (G)	F. Haber (G)
1919	J. Stark (G)	Not awarded
1920	C.E. Guillaume (Swi)	W.H. Nernst (G)
1921	A. Einstein (G/Swi)	F. Soddy (GB)
1922	N. Bohr (D)	F.W. Aston (GB)
1923	R.A. Millikan (US)	F. Pregl (Au)
1924	K.M.G. Siegbahn (Swe)	Not awarded

1 - 1993

Physiology /Medicine	_Literature_	_Peace_
E.A. von Behring (G)	Sully Prudhomme (F)	J.H. Dunant (Swi)
		F. Passy (F)
R.Ross (GB)	Theodor Mommsen (G)	E. Ducommun (Swi)
		C.A. Gobat (Swi)
N.R. Finsen (D)	Björnstjerne Björnson (N)	W.R. Cremer (GB)
I.P. Pavlov (R)	Frédéric Mistral (F)	Institute of International
	José Echegaray (Sp)	Law, Ghent
R. Koch (G)	Henryk Sienkiewicz (Pol)	B.S.F. von Suttner (Au)
C. Golgi (I)	Giousè Carducci (I)	T. Roosevelt (US)
S. Ramón y Cajal (Sp)		
C.L.A. Laveran (F)	Rudyard Kipling (GB)	E.T. Moneta (I)
		L. Renault (F)
P. Ehrlich (G)	Rudolf Eucken (G)	K.P. Arnoldson (Swe)
I. Mečnikov (R)		F. Bajer (D)
E.T. Kocher (Swi)	Selma Lagerlöf (Swe)	A.M.F. Beernaert (B)
		P.H.B.B. d'Estournelles
		de Constant (F)
A. Kossel (G)	Paul Heyse (G)	Permanent International
		Peace Bureau, Berne
A. Gullstrand (Swe)	Maurice Maeterlinck (B)	T.M.C. Asser (NL)
		A.H. Fried (Au)
A. Carrel (F)	Gerhart Hauptmann (G)	E. Root (US)
C.R. Richet (F)	Rabindranath Tagore (In)	H. La Fontaine (B)
R. Bárány (Au)	Not awarded	Not awarded
Not awarded	Romain Rolland (F)	Not awarded
Not awarded	Verner v. Heidenstam (Swe)	Not awarded
Not awarded	Karl Gjellerup (D)	International Committee
	Henrik Pontaoppidan (D)	of the Red Cross,
		Geneva
Not awarded	Not awarded	Not awarded
J. Bordet (B)	Carl Spitteler (Swi)	T.W. Wilson (US)
S.A.S. Krogh (D)	Knut Hamsun (N)	L.V.A. Bourgeois (F)
Not awarded	Anatole France (F)	K.H. Branting (Swe)
		C.L. Lange (N)
A.V. Hill (GB)	Jacinto Benavente (Sp)	F. Nansen (N)
O.F. Meyerhof (G)		
F.G. Banting (Ca)	W.B. Yeats (Ir)	Not awarded
J.J.R. Macleod (Ca)		
W. Einthoven (NL)	Wladyslaw Reymont (Pol)	Not awarded

Year	Physics	Chemistry
1925	J. Franck (G) G. Hertz (G)	R.A. Zsigmondy (G)
1926	J.B. Perrin (F)	T. Svedberg (Swe)
1927	A.H. Compton (US) C.T.R. Wilson (GB)	H.O. Wieland (G)
1928	O.W. Richardson (GB)	A.O.R. Windaus (G)
1929	L.-V. de Broglie (F)	A. Harden (GB) H.K.A.S. von Euler- Chelpin (Swe)
1930	C.V. Raman (In)	H. Fischer (G)
1931	Not awarded	C. Bosch (G) F. Bergius (G)
1932	W. Heisenberg (G)	I. Langmuir (US)
1933	E. Schrödinger (Au) P.A.M. Dirac (GB)	Not awarded
1934	Not awarded	H.C. Urey (US)
1935	J. Chadwick (GB)	F. Joliot (F) I. Joliot-Curie (F)
1936	V.F. Hess (Au)	P.J.W. Debye (NL)
1937	C.J. Davisson (US) G.P Thomson (GB)	W.N. Haworth (GB) P. Karrer (Swi)
1938	E. Fermi (I)	R. Kuhn (G)
1939	E.O. Lawrence (US)	A.F.J. Butenandt (G) L. Ružička (Swi)
1940	Not awarded	Not awarded
1941	Not awarded	Not awarded
1942	Not awarded	Not awarded
1943	O. Stern (US)	G. de Hevesy (H)
1944	I.I. Rabi (US)	O. Hahn (G)
1945	W. Pauli (Au)	A.I. Virtanen (Fi)
1946	P.W. Bridgman (US)	J.B. Sumner (US) J.H. Northrop (US) W.M. Stanley (US)

Physiology /Medicine	_Literature_	_Peace_
Not awarded	G.B.Shaw (GB)	J.A. Chamberlain (GB)
		C.G. Dawes (US)
J.A.G.Fibiger (D)	Grazia Deledda (I)	A. Briand (F)
		G. Stresemann (G)
J. Wagner-Jauregg (Au)	Henri Bergson (F)	F. Buisson (F)
		L. Quidde (G)
C.J.H. Nicolle (F)	Sigrid Undset (N)	Not awarded
C. Eijkman (NL)	Thomas Mann (G)	F.B. Kellog (US)
F.G. Hopkins (GB)		
K. Landsteiner (Au)	Sinclair Lewis (US)	L.O.N. Söderblom (Swe)
O.H. Warburg (G)	Erik Axel Karlfeldt (Swe)	J. Addams (US)
		N.M. Butler (US)
C.S. Sherrington (GB)	John Galsworthy (GB)	Not awarded
E.D. Adrian (GB)		
T.H. Morgan (US)	Ivan Bunin (stateless)	N.R.L. Angell (GB)
G.H. Whipple (US)	Luigi Pirandello (I)	A. Henderson (GB)
W.P. Murphy (US)		
G.R. Minot (US)		
H. Spemann (G)	Not awarded	C. von Ossietzky (G)
H.H. Dale (GB)	Eugene O'Neill (US)	C. Saavedra Lamas (Ar)
A. Szent-Györgyi von	Roger Martin du Gard (F)	E.A.R.G. Cecil (GB)
Nagyrapolt (H)		
C.J.F. Heymans (B)	Pearl Buck (US)	Nansen International Office for Refugees, Geneva
G. Domagk (G)	F.E. Sillanpää (Fi)	Not awarded
Not awarded	Not awarded	Not awarded
Not awarded	Not awarded	Not awarded
Not awarded	Not awarded	Not awarded
E.A. Doisy (US)	Not awarded	Not awarded
H.C.P. Dam (D)		
J. Erlanger (US)	Johannes V. Jensen (D)	International Committee of the Red Cross, Geneva
H.S. Gasser (US)		
A. Fleming (GB)	Gabriela Mistral (Chile)	C. Hull (US)
E.B. Chain (GB)		
H.W. Florey (GB)		
H.J. Muller (US)	Hermann Hesse (Swi)	E.G. Balch (US)
		J.R. Mott (US)

Year	Physics	Chemistry
1947	Appleton (GB)	R. Robinson (GB)
1948	P.M.S. Blackett (GB)	A.W.K. Tiselius (Swe)
1949	H. Yukawa (J)	W.F. Giauque (US)
1950	C.F. Powell (GB)	O.P.H. Diels (FRG)
		K. Alder (FRG)
1951	J.D. Cockcroft (GB)	E.M. McMillan (US)
	E.T.S. Walton (Ir)	G.T. Seaborg (US)
1952	F. Bloch (US)	A.J.P. Martin (GB)
	E.M. Purcell (US)	R.L.M. Synge (GB)
1953	F. Zernike (NL)	H. Staudinger (FRG)
1954	M. Born (GB)	L.C. Pauling (US)
	W. Bothe (FRG)	
1955	W.E. Lamb (US)	V. du Vigneaud (US)
	P. Kusch (US)	
1956	W. Shockley (US)	C.N. Hinshelwood (GB)
	J. Bardeen (US)	N.N. Semenov (USSR)
	W.H. Brattain (US)	
1957	C.N. Yang (China)	A.R. Todd (GB)
	T.-D. Lee (China)	
1958	P.A. Cerenkov (USSR)	F. Sanger (GB)
	I.M. Frank (USSR)	
	I.J. Tamm (USSR)	
1959	E.G. Segrè (US)	J. Heyrovsk´y (Cz)
	O. Chamberlain (US)	
1960	D.A. Glaser (US)	W.F. Libby (US)
1961	R. Hofstadter (US)	M. Calvin (US)
	R.L. Mössbauer (FRG)	
1962	L.D. Landau (USSR)	M.F. Perutz (GB)
		J.C. Kendrew (GB)
1963	E.P. Wigner (US)	K. Ziegler (FRG)
	M. Goeppert-Mayer (US)	G. Natta (I)
	J.H.D. Jensen (FRG)	

Physiology /Medicine	_Literature_	_Peace_
C.F. Cori (US)	André Gide (F)	The Friends Service
G.T. Cori (US)		Council (GB)
B.A Houssay (Ar)		The American Friends
		Service Committee (US)
P.H. Müller (Swi)	T.S. Eliot (GB)	Not awarded
A.C. de Abreu Freire	William Faulkner (US)	J. Boyd Orr (GB)
Egas Moniz (Por)		
W.R. Hess (Swi)		
P.S. Hench (US)	Bertrand Russell (GB)	R. Bunche (US)
E.C. Kendall (US)		
T. Reichstein (Swi)		
M. Theiler (SA)	Pär Lagerkvist (Swe)	L. Jouhaux (F)
S.A. Waksman (US)	François Mauriac (F)	A. Schweitzer (F/G)
H.A. Krebs (GB)	Winston Churchill (GB)	G.C. Marshall (US)
F.A. Lipmann (US)		
J.F. Enders (US)	Ernest Hemingway (US)	Office of the UN High
T.H. Weller (US)		Commissioner for
F.C. Robbins (US)		Refugees, Geneva
A.H.T. Theorell (Swe)	Halldór Laxness (Ic)	Not awarded
A.F. Cournand (US)	J.R. Jiménez (Sp)	Not awarded
W. Forssmann (FRG)		
D.W. Richards Jr. (US)		
D. Bovet (I)	Albert Camus (F)	L.B. Pearson (Ca)
G.W. Beadle (US)	Boris Pasternak (USSR)	G. Pire (B)
E.L. Tatum (US)	(declined the prize)	
J. Lederberg (US)		
S. Ochoa (US)	Salvatore Quasimodo (I)	P.J. Noel-Baker (GB)
A. Kornberg (US)		
F.M. Burnet (Austr)	Saint-John Perse (F)	A.J. Luthuli (SA)
P.B. Medawar (GB)		
G. von Békésy (US)	Ivo Andric (Y)	D.H.A.C. Hammar-
		skjöld (Swe)
F.H.C. Crick (GB)	John Steinbeck (US)	L.C. Pauling (US)
J.D. Watson (US)		
M.H.F. Wilkins (GB)		
J.C. Eccles (Austr)	Giorgos Seferis (Gr)	International Committee
A.L. Hodgkin (GB)		of the Red Cross,
		Geneva
A.F. Huxley (GB)		League of Red Cross,
		Societies, Geneva

Year	Physics	Chemistry
1964	Ch.H. Townes (US)	D. Crowfoot Hodgkin (GB)
	N.G. Basov (USSR)	
	A.M. Prochorov (USSR)	
1965	S.-I. Tomonaga (J)	R.B. Woodward (US)
	J. Schwinger (US)	
	R.P. Feynman (US)	
1966	A. Kastler (F)	R.S. Mulliken (US)
1967	H.A. Bethe (US)	M. Eigen (FRG)
		R.G.W. Norrish (GB)
		G. Porter (GB)
1968	L.W. Alvarez (US)	L. Onsager (US)
1969	M. Gell-Mann (US)	D.H.R. Barton (GB)
		Hassel (N)
1970	H. Alfvén (Swe)	L. Leloir (Ar)
	L. Néel (F)	
1971	D. Gabor (GB)	G. Herzberg (Ca)
1972	J. Bardeen (US)	Ch. B. Anfinsen (US)
	L.N. Cooper (US)	S. Moore (US)
	J.R. Schrieffer (US)	H. Stein (US)
1973	L. Esaki (J)	E.O. Fischer (FRG)
	I. Giaever (US)	G. Wilkinson (GB)
	B.D. Josephson (GB)	
1974	M. Ryle (GB)	P.J. Flory (US)
	A. Hewish (GB)	
1975	A. Bohr (D)	J.W. Cornforth (GB)
	B. Mottelson (D)	V. Prelog (Swi)
	J. Rainwater (US)	
1976	B. Richter (US)	W.N. Lipscomb (US)
	S.C.C Ting (US)	
1977	P.W. Anderson (US)	I. Prigogine (B)
	F. Mott (GB)	
	J.H. Van Vleck (US)	
1978	P.L Kapitsa (USSR)	P. Mitchell (GB)
	A.A. Penzias (US)	
	R.W. Wilson (US)	
1979	S.L. Glashow (US)	H.C. Brown (US)
	A. Salam (Pak)	G. Wittig (FRG)
	S. Weinberg (US)	

Physiology / Medicine	*Literature*	*Peace*
K. Bloch (US) F. Lynen (FRG)	Jean-Paul Sartre (F) (declined the prize)	M.L. King (US)
F. Jacob (F)	Mikhail Sholokhov (USSR)	United Nations' Childrens Fund (UNICEF)
A. Lwoff (F) J. Monod (F)		
P. Rous (US) C.B. Huggins (US)	Shmuel Y. Agnon (Is) Nelly Sachs (G)	Not awarded
R. Granit (Swe) H.K. Hartline (US) G. Wald (US)	Miguel A. Asturias (Guat)	Not awarded
R.W. Holley (US) H.G. Khorana (US) M.W. Nirenberg (US)	Yasunari Kawabata (J)	R. Cassin (F)
M. Delbrück (US) A.D. Hershey (US) S.E. Luria (US)	Samuel Beckett (Ir)	International Labour O. Organisation, Geneva
B. Katz (GB) U. von Euler (Swe) J. Axelrod (US)	Alexander Solsjenitsyn (USSR)	N.E. Borlaug (US)
E.W. Sutherland (US) G.M. Edelman (US) R.R. Porter (GB)	Pablo Neruda (Chile) Heinrich Böll (FRG)	W. Brandt (FRG) Not awarded
K. von Frisch (FRG) K. Lorenz (Au) N. Tinbergen (GB)	Patrick White (Austr)	H.A. Kissinger (US) Le Duc Tho (V) (declined the prize)
A. Claude (B) C. de Duve (B) G.E. Palade (US)	Eyvind Johnson (Swe) Harry Martinson (Swe)	S. MacBride (Ir) E. Sato (J)
D. Baltimore (US) R. Dulbecco (US) H.M. Temin (US)	Eugenio Montale (I)	A. Sakharov (USSR)
B.S. Blumberg (US) D.C. Gajdusek (US) R. Guillemin (US) A. Schally (US) R. Yalow (US)	Saul Bellow (US) Vicente Aleixandre (Sp)	M. Corrigan (GB) B. Williams (GB) Amnesty International N.
W. Arber (Swi) D. Nathans (US) H.O. Smith (US)	Isaac B. Singer (US)	M. Begin (Is) A. Sadat (Eg)
A.M. Cormack (US) G.N. Hounsfield (GB)	Odysseus Elytis (Gr)	Mother Teresa (In)

Year	Physics	Chemistry
1980	J.W. Cronin (US) V.L. Fitch (US)	P. Berg (US) W. Gilbert (US) F. Sanger (GB)
1981	N. Bloembergen (US) A.L. Schawlow (US) K.M. Siegbahn (Swe)	K. Fukui (J) R. Hoffmann (US)
1982	K.G. Wilson (US)	A. Klug (GB)
1983	S. Chandrasekhar (US) W.A. Fowler (US)	H. Taube (US)
1984	C. Rubbia (I) S. van der Meer (NL)	B. Merrifield (US)
1985	K. von Klitzing (FRG)	H.A. Hauptman (US) J. Karle (US)
1986	E. Ruska (FRG) G. Binnig (FRG) H. Rohrer (Swi)	D.R. Herschbach (US) Y.T. Lee (US) J.C. Polanyi (Ca)
1987	J.G. Bednorz (FRG) K.A. Müller (Swi)	D.J. Cram (US) J.-M. Lehn (F) C.J. Pedersen (US)
1988	L.M. Lederman (US) Schwartz (US) J. Steinberger (US)	J. Deisenhofer (FRG) R. Huber (FRG) H. Michel (FRG)
1989	N.F. Ramsey (US) H.G. Dehmelt (US/Ca) W. Paul (FRG)	S. Altman (US) T.R. Cech (US)
1990	J.I. Friedman (US) H.W. Kendall (US) R.E. Taylor (Ca)	E.J. Corey (US)
1991	P.-G. de Gennes (F)	R.R. Ernst (Swi)
1992	G. Charpak (F)	R.A. Marcus (US)
1993	R.A. Hulse (US) J.H. Taylor (US)	K.B. Mullis (US) M.Smith (Ca)

Physiology /Medicine	Literature	Peace
B. Benacerraf (US)	Czeslaw Milosz (Pol/US)	A. Perez Esquivel (Ar)
J. Dausset (F)		
G.D. Snell (US)		
D.H. Hubel (US)	Elias Canetti (GB)	Office of the UN High
R.W. Sperry (US)		Commissioner for
T.N. Wiesel (Swe)		Refugees, Geneva
S. Bergström (Swe)	Gabriel García Márquez (Co)	A. Myrdal (Swe)
B.I Samuelsson (Swe)		A. García Robles (M)
J.R. Vane (GB)		
B. McClintock (US)	William Golding (GB)	L. Walesa (Pol)
N.K. Jerne (D)	Jaroslav Seifert (Cz)	D. Tutu (SA)
G.J.F. Köhler (FRG		
C. Milstein (GB/Ar)		
M.S. Brown (US)	Claude Simon (F)	Intern. Physicians
J.L. Goldstein (US)		for the Prevention
		of Nuclear War
S. Cohen (US)	Wole Soyinka (Ni)	E. Wiesel (US)
R. Levi-Montalcini (I/US)		
S. Tonegawa (J)	Joseph Brodsky (US)	O. Arias Sánchez (CR)
J.W. Black (GB)	Naguib Mahfouz (Eg)	United Nations' M.
G.B. Elion (US)		Peace-Keeping Forces
G.H. Hitchings (US)		
J.M. Bishop (US)	Camilo José Cela (Sp)	The 14th Dalai Lama
H.E. Varmus (US)		(Tenzin Gyatso) (T)
J.E. Murray (US)	Octavio Paz (M)	M. Gorbachev (USSR)
E.D. Thomas (US)		
E. Neher (G)	Nadine Gordimer (SA)	Aung San Suu Kyi
B. Sakmann (G)		(Burma)
E.H. Fischer (US-Swi)	Derek Walcott (St. Lucia)	R. Menchú Tum (Guat)
E.G. Krebs (US)		
R.J. Roberts (GB)	Toni Morrison (US)	F.W. de Klerk (SA)
P.A. Sharp (US)		N. Mandela (SA)

The Bank of Sweden Prize in Economic Sciences in Memory of Alfred Nobel, List of Laureates

1969   R. Frisch (N)1975
        J. Tinbergen (NL)
1970   P. Samuelson (US)
1971   S. Kuznets (US)
1972   J.R. Hicks (GB)
        K. Arrow (US)
1973   W. Leontief (US)
1974   G. Myrdal (Swe)
        F.A. von Hayek (GB)
1975   L.V. Kantorovich (USSR)
        T.C. Koopmans (US)
1976   M. Friedman (US)
1977   B. Ohlin (Swe)
        J. Meade (GB)
1978   H. Simon (US)
1979   A. Lewis (GB)
        T.W. Schultz (US)
1980   L. Klein (US)
1981   J. Tobin (US)
1982   G.J. Stigler (US)
1983   G. Debreu (US)
1984   R. Stone (GB)
1985   F. Modigliani (US)
1986   J.M. Buchanan Jr. (US)
1987   R.M. Solow (US)
1988   M. Allais (F)
1989   T. Haavelmo (N)
1990   H.M. Markowitz (US)
        M. Miller (US)
        W.F. Sharpe (US)
1991   R. Coase (GB)
1992   G.S. Becker (US)
1993   R.W. Fogel (US)
        D.C. North (US

Abbreviations

Ar Argentina; Austr Australia; Au Austria;
B Belgium; Ca Canada; Co Colombia;
CR Costa Rica; Cz Czechoslovakia; D
Denmark; Eg Egypt; Fi Finland; F France;
FRG Federal Republic of Germany;
G Germany; (before 1948 and after 1990);
GB Great Britain; Gr Greece; Guat
Guatemala; H Hungary; Ic Iceland;
In India; Ir Ireland; Is Israel; I Italy;
J Japan; M Mexico; NL Netherlands;
Ni Nigeria; N Norway; Pak Pakistan;
Pol Poland; Por Portugal; R Russia;
(between 1922 and 1991 USSR); Sp Spain;
Swe Sweden; Swi Switzerland;
SA Union of South Africa; T Tibet;
US United States; V Vietnam;
Y Yugoslavia.

References

Albert Schweitzer - Folke Edsmyr, 1976.

Alfred Bernhard Nobel - Kenne Fant, 1991.

Alfred Nobel - Hellberg/Jonsson, 1984.

Churchill - Alan Moorhead, 1960.

Dynamitkungen - Rune Pär Olofsson, 1990.

Mother Teresa - Navin Chawla, 1992.

The Ascent of Man - J. Bronowski, 1973.

Nobelpristagarna - Sureförlaget, 1969.

Nobelpristagarna 1901-1991 - Förlags AB Wiken Bokförlaget.

Bra Böcker, 1991.

The Nobel Foundation's Statutes and Regulations, 1990.

Nobel Foundation Annual Report, 1992.

Slump och geni i vetenskapens värld - Fernand Lot, 1956.